The Little Book of HONESTY

By Zack Bush and Laurie Friedman
Illustrated by Vitor Lopes

THIS BOOK BELONGS TO:

_____

Copyright © 2023 Publishing Power, LLC
All Rights Reserved
All inquiries about this book can be sent
to the author at info@thelittlebookof.com
Published in the United States by Publishing Power, LLC
ISBN: 978-1-959141-15-0
For more information, visit our website:
www.BooksByZackAndLaurie.com
Paperback

What exactly is **HONESTY?** Maybe you've heard of it, but you're not quite sure what it means. Don't worry. You're not alone!

There's lots to know about what it means to be **HONEST.**
Ready to learn more? Just turn the page!

Being **HONEST** means being truthful—not only with your words but with your actions too.

Why is it important to be **HONEST?**

Because people learn to **TRUST** you when you make it a habit to always tell the **TRUTH** and do the **RIGHT** thing.

Here's an example of how it works... let's say you accidentally break something.

You have two options. You can be **HONEST** and tell the **TRUTH.** Or you can be **DISHONEST** and tell a **LIE.**

If you tell a **LIE**, that person will not only be upset you broke something, but they will also be unhappy you were not **HONEST**.

It is not always easy to be **HONEST**, but it is the only way that you can build **TRUST** with your family, teachers, and friends.

When you know that the people you care about **TRUST** you, you will feel good inside. You will even sleep better at night.

Being **HONEST** not only means telling the **TRUTH**, it also means acting **HONESTLY.**

Being HONEST means . . .

Not taking something that does not belong to you.

And returning something if it is not yours.

STEALING = Taking things that do not belong to you.

Being **HONEST** means doing your own work in school.

CHEATING = Doing something dishonest and unfair to others.

This is important because when you work hard, you will learn new things and grow.

Being **HONEST** also means following the rules and playing fairly.

When you do, you will feel good and have fun, and your friends and teammates will want to keep playing with you.

Another way to practice being **HONEST** is by **NOT** saying things about other people that are **UNTRUE.**

When you share your real ideas, thoughts, and feelings with others, you are talking HONESTLY.

But if you talk about other people, this is called GOSSIP, and it is a bad thing to do.

WHY? Because when you repeat something you heard that is UNTRUE, you could hurt someone's feelings, or even embarrass them.

A good rule to follow is to always treat others how you would like to be treated.

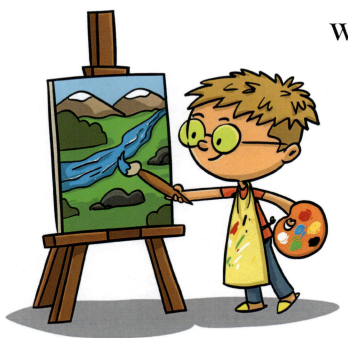

When you are being HONEST and telling the TRUTH, you should try your best to do it in a kind way.

LET'S SAY YOU PAINT A PICTURE AND ARE PROUD OF IT.

BUT WHEN YOU SHOW IT TO YOUR FRIEND, HE SAYS HE DOES NOT LIKE IT AND HE LAUGHS. THAT IS AN UNKIND RESPONSE.

YOU COULD ALSO HAVE AN UNKIND RESPONSE, LIKE TELLING YOUR FRIEND HE STINKS.

OR YOU COULD HAVE AN HONEST BUT KIND RESPONSE, LIKE TELLING YOUR FRIEND HE HURT YOUR FEELINGS.

Which response do you think is better?

Being **HONEST** but kind takes practice.
The more you do it, the better you will be at it!

Here's a trick to help:

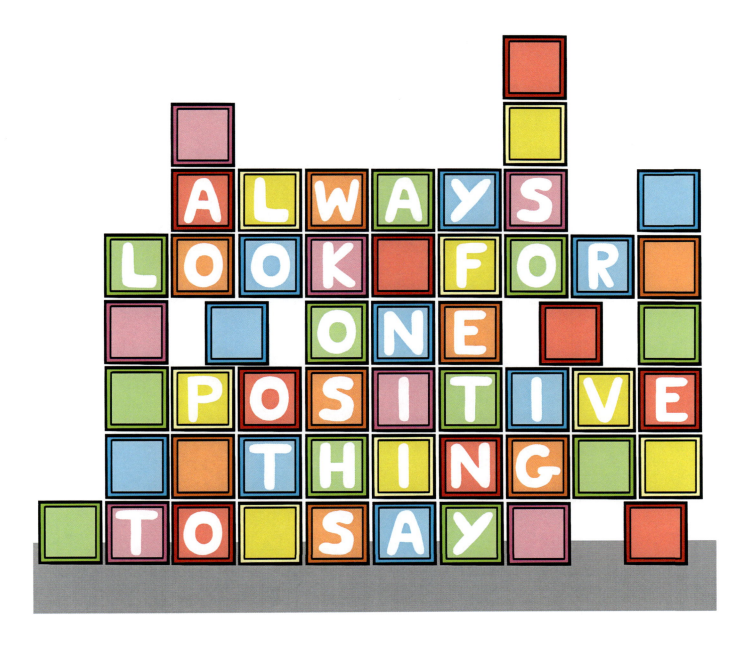

Here's an example: Maybe someone gives you a birthday present that you don't like. Telling that person you don't like the present is **HONEST**, but it is not kind.

An **HONEST** but kind response would be to thank that person for the present and tell them you are glad they came to your party.

Here's another example: Your friend gets a new pair of colorful sneakers. He loves them but you don't.

Telling him you do not like her sneakers is **HONEST**, but it is not kind.

An **HONEST** but kind response would be to tell your friend that you love seeing the big happy smile he has when he's wearing his new sneakers.

HONESTY is also about being real with yourself and others about who you are, what you want, and what you need.

Being **HONEST** with yourself isn't always easy.

Sometimes it takes some time to figure out what you are thinking and feeling. That is normal and perfectly okay.

Remember, you will always feel better when you talk to someone you **TRUST.**

There are so many good reasons to be **HONEST.**
You will . . .

EARN TRUST.

Inspire others.

FEEL PROUD.

STRENGTHEN RELATIONSHIPS.

Lessen stress.

SMILE MORE!

CONGRATULATIONS!
Now you know so much about what it means to be **HONEST.**

Here's your **HONESTY** badge.
Go ahead. Print it out, pin it on, and wear it proudly.

Go to the website
www.BooksByZackAndLaurie.com
and print out your badges from
the Printables & Activities page.

And if you like this book, please go to Amazon and leave a kind review.

Keep reading all of the books in #thelittlebookof series to learn new things and earn more badges.

Other books in the series include:

SOCIAL/EMOTIONAL/VALUES
The Little Book of Kindness
The Little Book of Patience
The Little Book of Confidence
The Little Book of Positivity
The Little Book of Love
The Little Book of Responsibility
The Little Book of Curiosity
The Little Book of Gratitude
The Little Book of Friendship
The Little Book of Laughter
The Little Book of Creativity
The Little Book of Imagination

ACTIVITIES/IDEAS
The Little Book of Camping
The Little Book of Sports
The Little Book of Music
The Little Book of Government

The Little Book of the Supreme Court
The Little Book of Transportation
The Little Book of Presidential Elections
The Little Book of Grandparents
The Little Book of Bedtime
The Little Book of Good Manners
The Little Book of Good Deeds
The Little Book of Dance
The Little Book of Yoga

SCIENCE/NATURAL WORLD
The Little Book of Nature
The Little Book of Outer Space
The Little Book of Going Green
The Little Book of Weather
The Little Book of Pets
The Little Book of Dinosaurs

MILESTONES/HOLIDAYS
The Little Book of Kindergarten
The Little Book of First Grade
The Little Book of Valentine's Day
The Little Book of Father's Day
The Little Book of Halloween
The Little Book of Giving (Holiday Edition)
The Little Book of Santa Claus

Made in United States
North Haven, CT
15 November 2023